FEVER COAT

CINDY KING

POETRY

ISBN 978-1-949540-37-6

C&R Press
crpress.org

Praise for Fever Coat

Like the goddess of war and wisdom sprung from her father's head, Cindy King has the power and poise of Athena. *Fever Coat* is reckless but not heedless, whip-smart but not slick. It takes risks including the greatest risk of being funny while also being piercing, devastating. It's a romp and a sob in the street. She is someone who has an intimate acquaintance with sorrow and pain and persistence. There's a "grimace behind (her) grin." Her critical, cold eye on American culture "Where everything, even butterflies, like cats and cattle, is belled" is clinical and caustic. I find the range and awareness–she misses nothing–to be extraordinary. This book will take you to school to learn about tenderness and retribution and a kind of revolution of feeling that would otherwise be amorphous or corrosive. "There's a lesson here," as she says, and it's about how King's skill and transformative powers can make a compelling work of art.
—Bruce Smith

Cindy King's *Fever Coat* has the delirious patina of a quantum nocturne troubled by personification, by what it means to be a person and how the world tries to unperson us. These poems are Cubist elegies beset by nightmares of transit where the Unicorn Tapestry erupts from the fabric, sketches of the mythological transformations that happen when we finally can decode the thin script of the dead languages of houseplants and read the star charts in the weak slant of the night refrigerator light.
—Simeon Berry

How rare to find poems as constantly surprising as those in *Fever Coat*. It's as if King's put Creation itself on "shuffle," so that we never know what's coming next. From jokes to Genesis, Rembrandt to rap, this book aims at nothing less than all the world, giving us what Shakespeare called "infinite variety." But the effect is not chaos, not white noise, but the consolation of witness, the solace of speech, of letting pain be spoken. "Even porcupines grow in wombs," she writes, and in King's hands even calamity can be cradled into a kind of peace, can perhaps be coaxed to crack a smile.

For all their playful–and painful–panache, all their riotous fun, these po- ems confront us with the most primordial questions: How can we under- stand ourselves, or communicate with each other? Is the world we find ourselves in just and holy, "or is it / the sight of a catastrophe?" King has no answers, but no great poet ever does. She reminds us that such ques- tions need to be lived in, lived through. Yes, ours is a world of change and flux, of fear and grief, but the best of these poems prove that the complexity of life can shine if lit by the right kinds of attention. For days when we feel like "the world's mostly tweetups, irreconcilable / differenc- es, legal separations, and restraining orders," *Fever Coat* becomes a call to resist all that, a call to make our own life, to find–in Frost's phrase–our own momentary stays against confusion.

—Michael Lavers

FEVER COAT

CONTENTS

Leverets

Night Shift

I start listening to houseplants,
learn their dead languages.
A fly lands in my soup
and I eat around it
until the bowl is empty.
Everyone loses something eventually.
My neck carries the weight of my head,
buckling with the thoughts that live there.
The withered mouth of
the philodendron
smiling broadly.
In the middle of the night
I replace the batteries
of the TV remote
that has been so faithful
and patient with me.
Across the alley in the shop
of the garment maker,
a hundred hands stitch trim
onto jackets, sew sleeves
to shoulders, steam creases
and seams. While I lie awake
in television light,
waiting for the night to end,
and for the third-shift mothers
to be returned to their children.

Noumenon

The bed was thus, the curtains were therefore.
The moon floated past the window frame
and appeared to be. Fans roared as softly as.
A blue light becoming, or a wind
unlike anything outside.
Or a memory of, but less than.
In other words, a fine dust settling on the dust ruffle.
Released from memory. Released into remembering.
Motor coach and reservoir, children and fools.
The pasture being itself, in other words, midnight, perfume.
Schopenhauer breathing into a paper bag.
Sequins, rutabaga, emerald hills.
Burj Khalifa and a feeling
that in a moment anything could.
That the clouds might.
4:00 p.m. Al Ain: what to say?
Or your voice, the risk of. And rebar.
Then traffic, rushing as if it could stop.
Sure it could.
The noise, the ticking. Noise,
noise, boom. You letting go
was unlike. You leaving
was nearly like.

Misdirection

> When love is gone, there's always justice.
> And when justice is gone, there's always force.
> And when force is gone, there's always Mom. Hi Mom!
>
> —Laurie Anderson

Nevertheless, the tooth my brother placed
beneath his pillow remained, all night,
and the next, and the one after that, unmoved.
Ditto for the milk and cookies we left for Santa.
Untouched. Unanswered. Return to sender.
Flash forward: After the earthquake, my brother
inspects an overpass for structural damage, and
I meet with a student approximately 1,986 miles away.
He's failing my class, he says, because he's cheating on his girlfriend.
Meanwhile, the governor of Alabama (initially advocating for a surgical
        approach)
signs a bill calling for chemical castration.
Next up: sterilization for deadbeat dads?

So yeah, there's still no light in the attic. But no worries,
the fire's burning on the other side of the house;
the water has only risen to the windows (the tornado's *waaay* down the
        street).
At the zoological museum, there's a scorpion suspended
in amber. Could it wait another millennium to sting?
As for the rats, ticks, and roaches, we could just as well see those at
        home.
Of extinction, what's not to love?
Who will mourn the pubic lice

in the ongoing war against body hair?
Could it be that it all boils down to what Laurie
Anderson said about love and justice? Like the last time
I saw my father on a gurney behind glass. Or the way I refuse
Communion: fingers curled into fists, arms crossed,
x-ing out the thumping thing that failed him
but is keeping me alive.

Figure & Ground

My mother always dreamt
of being a nurse, and she is,
I guess, in her own way. Upstairs,
folding our bedsheets into neat
hospital corners, smoothing
everything over, everything down.

It's fall and I should be in school,
but I haven't forgotten the lessons
of those first weeks of September
in silence and stillness,
and how to be unseen.

My father has just stitched
the gash in his hand.
The crooked smile
in his palm is what I'll remember,
his indifference and the blood.

While the young bull still
tramples flowerbeds,
lazily chewing the last of the petunias,
tail swishing at horseflies.

By this time next year
he'll hang in the garage
from the hook next to my bicycle,
tongue, pink, spilling
like streamers from handlebars.

My father shouts to my mother
in the weak refrigerator light.
I know he is in want
of something he already has.
I think of him as an illusion—
sometimes a face, at others
a wineglass.
My mother of the magic
eye sees past his surface,
to something that no matter how long
or close I look, I'm blind to.

I am anxious for his early retirement
to the recliner, for quiet and closed doors,
for snoring.
It will be years before I decode his rage,
decades until I see it in myself and learn
to smooth it over, to smooth it down.

Anamnesis

I remember the last time I had fish.
It was at a waterfront restaurant
with my mother.
I ordered a cocktail.
My mother brought her own—
a pharmacological rainbow
she shook from what looked to me
like a little plastic coffin.
It was a Saturday or Sunday
when the fish was placed before me,
and when I ran my knife down
the silver length of its body,
it opened its mouth.
Sit up straight, I heard it say,
and *elbows off the table*—
though that was decades ago
and it could have come
from my mother's mouth.
My mother is a fish now, like
the one in the Faulkner novel.
You are what you eat, they say.
I have become a vegetarian
instead of becoming my mother.

Elegy for a Eulogy

You asked me to deliver the eulogy
at Dad's memorial service
to spare the survivors of our family
the mortifying prospect of public speaking.
For five hours, I have flown above earth,
wordlessly, over Great Plains and Rocky Mountains.
Under a moon of reading light, I have learned
why no one ever calls it a light by which to write.
I have failed the galaxy, didn't listen to the stars.

I would have rather bought more lilies
than to say what I remember,
brought another noodle casserole.
Let me rummage instead through your pantry, Mom,
tear wild violets from your yard.
But please, don't ask me to see him from a distance,
to view him with a naked eye, to show
him as a moon, without blemish,
free of rilles, scars, dark sides.

Animus

When I imagine my dad in the afterlife
I think of him haggling with the ferryman,
refusing the ride across the river
and choosing instead to swim.
At the gates of heaven, he won't
give his name, demands to speak
with God himself, as if God were
the general manager, the senior
supervisor of the universe.
On the muddy banks
of the river of forgetfulness,
he chugs the murky water.
I wonder if in here, in the hereafter,
he still remembers me.

I'm not sure what the animals think
when they see him in his stiff white coat,
wandering the fields of Elysium.
Do they sniff the air and trot away coolly
or come to lick his palm?
A long look, I should think,
could call beasts back into the wild,
drive out any trace of domestication.
What words would they have for the man
who butchered them,
whose sacrifice filled our family's plates—
rosy ham, leg of lamb bouquet?
What lessons might I learn
in magnanimity and forgiveness?

Spiritus

It woke me again last night,
the dream of the river we
swam in as kids
in view of our parents and grandparents,
our cousins, aunts, and uncles.
It was all dried up, the river,
river stones and dirt
like a cobbled road to ruin.
A canopy of bare
branches rattled in dust,
powdered by January wind.

I couldn't see you but
felt you were there, found
instead, in this landscape
we know, a drum aflame
with tiger lilies.
And run aground in a bank
of sand, the broken back
of a wicker chair, antiquity
of a lost way of life.

Now, as I stand in your basement
on a ladder under the raw light
of an unshaded bulb,
I think of you, and flatten
my hands on the wall of
cardboard boxes
as if to say *stop*, to steady
myself against memory.

A spider spins a web in the corner:
invitation, warning, I can't comprehend.
No lesson or revelation,
just brown boxes, appendixes
of a concluded life.
When I speak to you in dreams
you can never hear me and don't reply.
I stand and watch the spider
who also says nothing.
Time sweeps unnoted across the clock face.
The sump pump kicks on and the boiler.
And something moves the air at the nape
of my neck and forehead, and a few strands
fall into my eyes.

Corpus

When you finish burning, what's left
sends a black thread of smoke
through fresh ash like a hand
waving the last of us away.
You didn't ask to return.
If you did, God never answered,
passing your request to some minor deity,
some lesser bird of paradise.
Nonetheless, you're here,
your body the shape of a milk snake,
whale shark, dust devil—
something only appearing to be dangerous.
Alive, we knew you as a closed door,
the sound of crushed gravel, a truck
backing down the drive. For how long
did I mistake you for night,
a dog's bark, an owl?
Now, we've packed up cold cuts,
hung dress clothes, and didn't sing.
Though we'd rather sleep,
we drink whisky in the backyard.
But still, here you are, failed storm,
waterspout, empty threat that's not quite done with us.

Mortality Forward, Mortality on the Nose

Sunshine. Everyday, sun. A thrust through
the turnstile to the unforgiving heaven, desert of forgetting—
your childhood, adolescence, most of your adult life.

The walk in the park, not much mortality in that.
You need fitness—heart, lungs, abs.
The other list: cigarettes, antidepressants, box wine,
all those micro-mortalities accumulate in the bloodstream.

Didn't you ask? You didn't ask. My father died last year.
He was a butcher; Hell is for vegans.
Those pink rocks look just like pork chops.
I know all about his *I-told-you-so's*, nothing of your *I'm-so-sorries*.

I keep walking in sunshine. No prophesies
required. No sunscreen or shade.
Crosswalk. White light. Man made of stars.
The RV that nearly hit me. *Murderers*,
I shout from the middle of the street.
Oh, if only I had a teenager to be ashamed of
me, to see his mother, sultana in cheap sneakers.

My father used to say, *Clean your plate. God put animals on earth for us to eat.*
Who's eating them now? What's eating him?

God, what gives? Cleanliness isn't godliness anymore.
Is there a he, she, or it (anyone) at the end of this goddamned prayer line?
My dad, he'd pick up if he had a phone down there.
As it was, his last pro-mortality, a burger he ate
with my ghost child. Offspring of a nine-month pregnancy scare,
eating with my father.

Fear is to rage what blade is to whetting stone,
shame the utensil he most avoided.
Regret a carcass dismembered.

Drumstick, music, with something he'd fill my plate.
My mother tells me he wasn't drafted, he
enlisted in the army at the height of the War.
He wanted to kill, she says.
He wanted to go to college.

Soft Skills

As a partner—then spouse, you only made it
three years. At most, it was an implausible
part to play. Bills piled up faster than
you could pay them, as did clothes and dirty dishes.
Transgressions came quicker than apologies.
Resentment settled over you like a thick layer of dust.
You could, however, shake a tambourine,
bash cymbals together between your knees.
Percussion, they were the very definition:
the striking of one solid object against another
with some degree of force.
Nevertheless, you could still keep time.
From dusk until dawn, you could wait for meteor showers,
could traverse the universe for days
without ever leaving the sofa.
As Aphrodite, you bribed and cheated, were
responsible for war (contributing cause, mostly, but who can say?).
Like Eurydice, you learned to never turn and look backward.
Blindly ambitious, you could moonwalk on stilts.
Festooned with rickrack and feathers,
you were an aspiring craft-*astrophe.*
All night, with hands tied behind,
you could accompany Bach on the triangle,
could cha-cha-cha, your feet never missing a beat.
Night and day, you were a one-woman rodeo,
a twelve-screen megaplex unto yourself.
You were beyond recrimination.
You held vigils for jokes that failed to make anyone laugh.
Stood up for sinking ships and whatever else was going down.
Rallied for the optimists whose causes weighed less than bird bone.

For the lust-struck and lonely, you sang torch songs.
You started a petition for motherless bullfrogs.
You disassembled matriarchal despair
and rebuilt it as a bulldozer.
You put together puzzles, gave others
the satisfaction of placing the final piece.
You twisted giraffes from balloons
and offered them to children,
wrapped your arms around an entire city and
squeezed out most of its suffering.

But as a partner—then spouse, you only made it three years.
      As a partner and spouse, you failed.

Hard Truths

You saw me stand to hold the present
against the past, subtracting what happened
from what didn't. The cat and dog
chase each other's tails. A key turns
in the lock after midnight.

Homecoming and going. The start of a new day,
nothing more. Scrape breakfast plates,
throw the rest into the trash. The sun springs
pink from a fresh wound.

Every dish washed is how I could never quit,
unless we ceased to eat altogether,
never rose from our beds to begin with.
To fear failure (and I fear it). I can never be
exactly what this household dreams of.
The door's lock houses our loneliness
and what inevitably comes for all of us.
Beyond the horizon and all I have scoured
is the latent potential, a neonatal possibility
of lies I tell you and ones I tell myself.

Possession

Open package

Remove Styrofoam

Discard Styrofoam

Do not eat Styrofoam

Keep staples from wrists

Keep staples from eyes

Remove all parts: base, top, shelves, dowels, anxiety, screws, nail holder, nails, rage, brackets, back panel, these instructions (you've done that), depression, espresso-colored stickers, cat standing on package

Place items on carpet (no carpet)

Place items on scratch-free surface (not beneath cat)

Gather shelves into one area

Gather hardware into another

Everything will appear to be hardware

Everything has potential to scratch

Find hammer

Keep hammer away from head

Keep hammer away from heads of others

Find screwdriver

Find it is the wrong kind

Cry into hands

Try not to cry into hands

Try not to cry

Try never to cry again

Attach sides to base with wooden dowels

(What are dowels?)

The only items from package made from actual wood

Withhold judgment

Attach top to base

See frame wobble

See frame collapse

Repeat previous steps

Not all steps, only those necessary

(What is necessary?)

That which eliminates wobble

That which prevents collapse

Do not eat Styrofoam

Keep staples from wrists

Force screws into predrilled holes

Not those predrilled holes

The other ones

Start by using fingers

Feel screws bite skin

Finish with screwdriver (still the wrong kind)

Unfold back panel

Yes, it is not one piece

Yes, it is held together with packing tape

Withhold judgment

Resist impulse to quit

Repress urge to give up

Use tape measure…

Search for tape measure…

Search for tape measure…

Search for tape measure…

Using your judgment (you may judge now)

Position back panel

Do not use tape

Attach to frame with nails at even intervals

Even intervals

Use nail holder

Not fingers

Use nail holder

There should be no leftover nails
(There are leftover nails)
Place shelf pins in predrilled holes
Yes, those holes
Shelves should not slope
Shelves should be even
Shelves should not slide out onto scratch-free surface
Position bookcase in bedroom
Unpack box labeled "Tom's Books"
Unpack box labeled "Mine"
Forget difference
Forget distinction
Shelve together
Books, bookshelves, espresso-colored stickers
Everything is yours

No Will

You won't be prepared for the probate lawyer,
who'll fail to find in his heart's budget
water or tissues for tears.
From all accounts in his economy, neither
has ever returned the beloved.

No one will mention the traffic downtown,
warn of five-car collisions, overturned
semis and minivans in flames.

At the justice end of Commerce Street,
they won't make it clear
that your car will be met with barricades.
No one will say where to park near the courthouse,
no mention of meters or need for change.

They won't say how you'll sleepwalk through sprinklers,
sink into earth by your heels.
It won't be disclosed why when crossing the street,
you can't be bothered to look both ways.

You won't know that you'll want to ask the man
behind yellow tape why he jumped
on *this* of all mornings, from *this* of all buildings
so near your destination.
You won't care to know the source of his suffering
or what could've been done to have stopped him.

You won't be told that the judge will be late—
no excuse or apology—

When he'll finally appear, nobody'll say
that you'll still be expected to rise.

No one will say of the courtroom,
it belongs in an old Hollywood film—
all polished wood and windows that span
from floor to ceiling.
The afternoon light won't be explained,
how it'll be softened by sheers.
No one will tell you you'll see nothing as beautiful,
like you did the time before.

Matrons of the Ward

A widow is sentenced up to fifteen years
after the departure of her beloved
to sleep with his clothes: the happier
the marriage, the more complete
her rehabilitation. Our institutions
aim to protect the public after all.
Iron Lady is a film about rust.
And the one on disarmament is *Annie Get Your Gun.*
The moon never asked for "Clair de Lune."
The moon was, well, famous before.
A woman must share her story as if every man
has lived it in the great, grand history of the world.
If only she could tell it in a way that those who heard it
would literally explode—or spark just a bit,
then leap overboard. Unremarkable still that a woman
has never been known for sawing a man in two. Or for freeing
herself from a straitjacket while chained to the floor of the ocean.

Neoteny

Daily Affirvotions

Those pains in your chest aren't a heart attack, it's that bra you've been wearing since high school.

No, you're not fat, your friend's just built like a runway model.

That face you glimpsed in the storefront window, don't worry, it wasn't yours (and of course they sell those jeans in your size).

You look old in that picture only because you're holding a newborn. But no, no worries, that baby's not yours.

You're not pregnant for at least five different reasons. And certainly not, no, not one of them is menopause.

That's just a pimple, a hangnail, an ordinary mole.

Did you forget, you left your place a mess? No, you haven't been burglarized.

No one has used your credit card in El Paso; no one's charged a slushy, a Slim Jim, and 50 cartons of Winstons.

Yes, you spellchecked that message, changed *shits* to *shirts* before clicking send. And that letter, yes, it had plenty of postage; the receiver has just chosen not to reply.

Your car is in park, parking brake on. It has not rolled through the garage door, down the driveway, and out into the quiet street. No, your headlights aren't on.

Those are white hydrangeas, not doctors staked in the bushes. No, that's a unicorn, not a police car.

Relax, no one's looking at you. That fine young gentleman's not staring, he sees right through, to the unicorn standing behind you,

and as for God, as for God you're good, God doesn't see you either.

Capacitor (Be Mine)

Call us anything: *spirits*, *specters*, *spooks*—
Say what you will about ghosts & widows:
that we don't exist, we're invisible,
that we go naked under the sheets,
and leave pornography in little free libraries.

Oh, how we messed with Ms. O'Keeffe
until she ditched mimesis for yonic flowers—
Sweet ruin of a decaying arrangement,
biological clock shocked by the red pulse of time...

Oh, how we would take your camera
and keep it on the nightstand
next to our bed. How we would take you
in your Subaru, between dashboard
and bucket seats—despite red dirt
and lousy music.

Serendipity, acne, nothing connecting to nothing.
Poltergeistly, wet-palmed, the mopey joy
of mumbling the same words
because they never come out quite right.

Pretty much everything moves at erosion speed;
those blemishes on the blue sky are called *clouds*.
The world's mostly tweetups, irreconcilable
differences, legal separations, and restraining orders.
Forever after, the taxes happily unprepared. Our backs
bent beautifully like the workers at fulfillment centers.

Everyone's always endorsing accuracy over precision—
closeness of the measurements to a specific value
over closeness of the measurements to each other.
Arrows missing hearts, bypassing bodies altogether.
(Would it help to get a bow?)
Or should we keep throwing them
and throwing, everly happy, everly after.

Flake

Yeah, there were things I didn't know,
like how you're not supposed to give newborns water,
run your car with the garage door closed.
How you're not supposed to drive 2,000 miles
on a spare tire, or how a lost filling
becomes a broken tooth, then no tooth at all.
And how loving someone to the exclusion
of all others is always a bad idea.
Like the joke hiding in the Rothko,
like the alarm clock in your neighbor's
apartment you hear each day at 6:00 a.m.
Don't put butter on a fever.
Starve a burn, feed an abstract expressionist.
Some truths are best untold.
The answer to the question is liverwurst.
Many a great man's face has been stamped
on currency that's now worthless.
Don't microwave melamine. It is an artifact of the 1960s.
I too am an artifact. Just as the pharaoh
became an artifact when he was lifted from sand.
And you're surprised he was autophobic
and buried with his concubines?
My heart is made of shale.
I heard a meadowlark singing and asked if she
would move in with me. She may have said yes
if it weren't for that thing with the alarm clock.
It would seem, dear sir, that my credit score precedes me.
It will end in lost deposits—and quite possibly tears.
That zero in my brain is being seduced by a one.
My brain became a slow jam.

Let's get it on.
Then it switched stations and was wrapped in a prophylactic.
I was fixing a sandwich at the time.
We're not just taxpayers, we're all roses!
My brain was kicked by another brain,
which I borrowed from my neighbor (not, for the record, Mr. 6:00 a.m.).
Does anyone else ever think that the heart's too near the armpits?
Love stinks.
All hail the woman of shale.
It's just me.
We all think the best of each other, don't we,
especially those with guns in their glove box.
Some day that whimper will become a bang,
at least that's what they tell me,
and it won't be so easy to drown it out
with 90 decibels of R&B.
Here's the least, save the date, let's make it official.
Check out this invisible ink.
Be on the lookout for the woman of shale.
Cross my heart, hope to die,
this time, I swear, she's not me.

Spring and All, Etc.

I once met a man
five blocks from my apartment
by pretending I was lost.
His hair smelled of spring rain.
Did you ever fall asleep standing up?
At some point, we all had tails.
Even porcupines grow in wombs.
Even my cat knows what she wants
and how to get it, despite her limited
vocabulary, even if that thing is nothing
at all and she becomes a bowling ball
dropped onto my mattress when I'm trying to sleep.
Spring: forsythias simmer, froth—percolate?
Rain decides upon whom it will fall. Cherry blossoms
spread their bawdy propaganda.
Do caterpillar skins pulse with phantom wings?
Cicadas outgrow themselves,
discard their bodies like souls.
What do trees care for love?
They split, distort initials and hearts
we carve into their bark.
Yet it seems they know something about revenge.
Like the man who left me for a Google map
and found his way to the museum, where he discovered
that dinosaurs traveled in packs (social animals after all)
and were not the lonely, cold-blooded carnivores we'd imagined.
Take my word for it. You need not believe me.
Just look for yourself and see that everything
is purring and trilling and everlastingly soul twinned.
I once was lost, now I'm blind.
Remember: you are who you own.

Any Other Name

This one goes out to Pizzazz Lee,
who says she got nothing from her daddy
but his bitch-ass last name. Whose mama
surrendered hers, was no longer *Mama*
but eight digits dressed in orange.
Pizzazz, who understood the rich girls
from our busted-up schoolbooks,
knew they'd never "run, Sally, run" with us,
even before she could read. Who
called her Barbie *BayBomb Sapphire*
and moved the Dreamhouse to Barbados,
named her pitbull *Pluto-nium*, because
"his shit could kill you" (he ain't no Disney dog).
Pizzazz, who'd never marry, who'd take no name from a no-name,
from the *Walkers, Parkers, Sleepers* of our neighborhood.
Who beat down boys for calling her *pizza, piazza,*
Or *pig'z azz Lee*. Pizzazz Lee, whenever she called to me,
she pistol-whipped my heart and hijacked my knees.

Know Your Place: Disco Edition

I feel really dumb at the nightclub
wearing pink vinyl pants with sensible shoes,
compression socks with a red velvet corset,
bifocals and borrowed biker jacket.
A bad place to bring a cat,
same goes for a headache.
Ditto for a cup of herbal tea
and a copy of the Old Testament.
A mirror ball rotates above the dance floor,
fracturing light into unholy pieces,
the perfect planet for narcissists
if it weren't too small for all of us
to make of it our home.

Happy Hour

I drank in the superficial darkness of a 4:30 twilight
and thought something would happen,
though nothing did.
I've never been known for my ability to see into the future.
This isn't to say I haven't got intuition.
It's possible I've been loitering too long
in the gingerbread kitchens of witches,
engaging in books with onionskin pages
and faulty spells for *happy* tears.
And then came a knock,
and then I ignored it.
And with a great deal of tenderness
I made peace with the door.
Could it be that I'm finally moving forward?
On my feet, cacti and foothills scrolling beside me,
but the ground where I stand remains still.
And with some clairvoyance, I see you on your feet,
legs moving you down a cobbled street in Paris or Bruges.
Though it could be that at this hour
you are sitting in your cinema of self-loathing,
playing and replaying a cringe reel:
> the great effort resulting in ridicule,
> the grand gesture that ended in rejection,
> the bold action that failed.
So, when you move it's with more noise than intended,
as if to flood the vast chasm of silence with sound,
like a witch in her kitchen—one younger, less warty,
who is shaking up a cocktail of alacrity and joy.

Behind the Wheel

The therapist asks me a question,
and I don't know the answer.
I suspect she knows because
she knows me better than
I know what's under the hood.
I have given her the keys
to my inner Ferrari, so she drives
recklessly down the treacherous
coastal highway of our weekly grand prix.
I open my mouth. No words.
My tongue backed into the garage
of my throat, where it idles,
then stalls and fails to turn over.
I hold a can to my lips
and hope that it is gasoline.
The therapist repeats the question,
and I lose control of my leg.
It skidders and shakes—no brakes
for the unbalanced thigh.
I stare at the door
like it's a windscreen,
see through to the receptionist,
buffing her fingernails
as if this were a body shop,
not one repairing heads.
Tonight, she'll be driving,
top down, with her friends,
where the answers bloom like wildflowers
beyond the road's soft shoulders.

Fault (After Harryette Mullen)

If only she would have…didn't she know that…she should have…why didn't she…how didn't she…how could she have…she was the only one who…she should have known not to… she just shouldn't have… she was way too…why wasn't she…she just didn't…what was she… where were her…how could she… she might have been…she didn't… how could she be so…didn't she realize…she just wasn't…she didn't understand that…how could she not have known that…why didn't she simply…she should have…if only…

Crescendo

Consent, however, there was never such a thing.
As if when a boy teased you, it only meant he liked you,
And if you teased back, you'd disappear. As if
being called *slut* made you taller,
and *whore* restored your voice—magic, see?
As if your fear of men could make you
walk on water, their touch could split you in half—
Long division (cherry pie filling), two selves never to meet again.
As if you could no longer breathe underwater,
surfacing no longer an option. You'd spit
and sputter and do the math. The equation adds up:
Asking for it + asking for it = deserving it. If A, then B.
Add. Subtract. Divide. Go forth, multiply.
Let them spin lead into gold,
speak secret names for God,
antiseptic, wind, water on your skin, eroding your hoodoo body…
It's all perfectly sane, normal even: predator/prey, Kingdom Animalia.
As if rape is never really rape,
as if you were quiet, quite quiet, then very, very loud.

Free to Speak

It sounds natural when I hear the anchorwoman say it, *bitch*,
on morning-talk-show TV. And quite normal from my sister
when she's shouting to our mother through the phone.
From my father, I must have heard it for the first time,
preceded by *son of a*, since women were beneath the dignity
of his insults or rage.
I remember the ex-lover who, when overcome with passion,
would whisper the word
right before his body's collision with mine.
I used to never say it aloud,
would skip the lyric in songs of old men and their money,
about girls who had gone too far.

But now, when the girls beneath my window call, *Hey, bitch,*
to their friends, I am unmoved.
No other word provokes in me such indifference.
You're my bitch, I repeat to my reflection, *You're my bitch,*
to keep me from forgetting I am mastered.
I am owned.

Resting Bitch Face

You know the one, the woman who's told to smile
to put the men in the boardroom at ease.
There's no difference between a blindfold and a gag,
bandage and tourniquet in the future.
Her face muscles fail in the first minute,
the corners of her mouth starting to sag
as her feelings betray her obedience.

When she allows herself to dream, she imagines a newborn
sunrise, a naked truth, thrust red and wailing
into the arms of each man.
Why does the woman smile inside the vast boardroom of history?
Because she is the blindfold, shielding the world's eyes
from patriarchal violence. She is the triage
for generational trauma shot at close range
through the heads of men.
She is both the bandage—you get it—and the gag.
She smiles with only half her face,
lips sealed, for now, over clenched teeth.

S.O.S.

On account of the grimace
behind my grin, I don't think
anyone trusts me.
Groaning, swaying, basement flooding,
inspector's clipboard's nightmare.
I have to say, I do
appear unhinged,
door, legally separated,
not yet divorced.
The host among dinner guests, the only
one who doesn't contract food poisoning.
Perv in the fitting room
huffing underwear while flipping the bird
to the two-way mirror.
(Who's the pervert here?)
Electrons pass through us, dark matter
slogging through dark mud. No surprise
the blizzard is jazzed to be a blizzard,
never again wanting to be water,
not even ice.
That kitten was born to be a meme.
The spray tan aspiring to be a household staple.
I can sometimes sit on my couch
and not know where it starts and I end.
I can stand by my refrigerator and fail
to see any difference.
You are what you own.
No wonder our prayers never
reach the stratocumulus ears of heaven.
Secular sacrament, blessed, sacred

clearance sale.

The jacaranda targeting my windshield,

all part of god's plan?

At last, a ship on the horizon!

It's heading toward the shore.

But catching sight of us, it

turns back into the blizzard,

the storm taking it into its mouth.

It's Either That, or You're Pregnant Again

A man gives a kidney because he doesn't believe
in God. Believes in Kickstarter, Facebook, Instagram,
in a copperhead coiled on the welcome mat.
There's a man dressed as Lincoln
in the delivery room. It's impossible
to know what the sniper needs,
but she's packing a sandwich anyway,
which is preferable, by far, to gnawing
at her nails. The differences between a baseball bat and a gavel,
like the difference between justice and revenge—nothing
like the difference between revenge and retribution.
No, not anything we have to think about.
The remains arrive and are ready to be picked up, as is
the tab from the city, and the eyefuls of stardust
and ice, blue-gray like an X-ray or ultrasound.
Rah, rah, Rauschenberg, they cheered at the opening.
Pages of answers as from a deposition or teacher's guide,
utterly unreadable at bedtime.
The men from the forensic lab examine the prints
expecting to find the Minotaur, or (at least)
a complete man. My dearest, darling afterward,
how I've tired of your song.
Let my conscience be your guide, the iridescent
scales of it drifting into your orbit. The pen is the greatest
predictor of the future. Perhaps now's the time
I should forgive my father.
This afternoon I have a feeling that my windshield
will shatter, and—can you imagine—*me*, bejeweled
in safety glass! The red carpet. All a-glitter,
expecting an award. Open the aperture

and say "ahh." Eleven years old and it's serious,
look at her figure and ground compelling conviction,
her laying bare of the device! She's crowning.
And you will come to an opening,
when you come to an opening,
take a deep breath, blink, then fully open your eyes.

Mis-

It's impossible to feed you when I can't find
your mouth, an inconvenience when you levitate
or pass though walls. How to coax a whale on the beach
back into water. How to rescue a jellyfish
without becoming one.
Forget what you learned in school
about silence and standing still, about
how a cricket is just a cockroach that sings.
When you discover the true source of your power,
you might be underwhelmed.
At the sight of bronze shoes, why weep?
The grief and loss meetups were never canceled
due to a lack of victims.
When you can't leave the house,
call Alexa, a woman with a machine
inside, or a machine with a woman inside,
I can't remember which.
She'll never say, "It takes one to know one,"
so I guess that means we're still human.
If you ask, she'll tell you that recovery
is a kind of motherhood,
where you are your own infant, your
birth a mere deliverance.

Lightbulb

This is the sight of a lightbulb
struggling to maintain its composure.
This is the sight of the Tooth Fairy
who is kicking my head, which makes sense,
because she exists only in my imagination.
This is the sight of starlight sent from a dying sun
that no one will ever see.
This is the sight of a lipstick message
scrawled on a shattered mirror.
This is the sight of an antelope
stopped at a suburban crosswalk.
This is the sight of kindness
through the lens of a microscope.
(Yes, it really is that small.)
This is the sight of a requiem
that has been diagnosed with terminal cancer.
This is the sight of the person
who scans the daily obituaries.
This is the sight of that same person
finding their own.
I love the sight of the oscillating fan
when it turns its attention on me.
This is the sight of the stomping upstairs
in the apartment directly above me.
This is the sight of a page turning,
which is the sight of a guilty man.
This is the sight of the driver, who,
if they didn't have to, wouldn't look at the road.
This is the sight of the open mouth,
gasping on a waterbed, where all the body's eyes

are shedding wistful tears.
This is the sight of the perfume that stalks
the scentless wrist.
This is the sight of a life jacket
rolling in the surf, or is it
the sight of a catastrophe?
This is the sight of the lightbulb bursting,
the sight of everyone aging all at once,
and of someone flipping through TV channels
searching for someone to be.
This is the sight of a fiddler on the roof,
which is also the sight of the new moon.
The goddess of war and wisdom sprung
from her father's head, so that the sight
of her birth was the origin of all bright ideas.

Blastema

A Poem by Dean Young by Mary Ruefle by Cindy King

Assume for decades
I haven't suffered a cataclysmic,
life-altering event. A pregnancy, a loss,
an assault of any kind. The dog
in the raincoat is a global phenomenon,
an international incident, a cosmic,
seismic event. Doesn't believe in anxiety,
doesn't believe in facial recognition software.
Assume I haven't seen bulls swabbed
onto cave walls. Assume I haven't tried the world's
most poisonous fish. Assume I have crushed,
then failed to resuscitate, the scorpion in my bathtub.
(I'm that kind of person.)
Assume I haven't burned an effigy of Renée Jeanne Falconetti.
Assume more than once I have sobbed in public places.
Of course, I've never painted a Pollock by numbers.
Many times have I never painted a Klein by the number
(the one corresponding with blue).
Never have I left a painting at your doorstep.
Never have I poured paint into your mouth.
Never have I died. Never, as a consequence, have I lived.
I'm sorry. No, I apologize. Someone told me
never to apologize for being late, but
to thank them, instead, for waiting.
Maybe now the neighboring countries
can live in peace and the dead can return
as starlings and gather in the evening sky.

Nuclear/Unclear

If you want to know how it feels,
try lifting with your back
instead of your knees. It's like using
the Port O Let and trying not to breathe.
Like being vegetarian and trying
to separate beans from beef. It's like
trying to read every headstone
at Arlington National Cemetery.
You'll pick up what I'm laying down
(just remember, lift from the knees)
when I say the life preserver is worthless
when the life in question isn't worth preserving.
It's unlikely that anyone like an American President
would say what the fascist dictator did.
When the dinosaurs knocked on your door
they only wanted their planet back,
doomsday documentarians
camping out in your browser's history.
About lifting with your back,
you get it, don't you?
A thought living outside the skull
is an action. The belief being that
when a victim, unconscious, stumbles
toward the light, the light is of little consequence,
and the muzzle is useless when the mouth
has little of consequence to say.

This Land Is Your Land, This Land Was Made for You

This land, land of the 12-ounce pound cake,
Of billboards with fine print (taxes, fees, batteries not included).
This home, home of those who wish to shop local, and
to do it are willing to drive the extra mile.
Home of those who take elevators at the gym
to StairMasters on the second floor.
This place of face-mask hoarders
(freedom from want)
who now refuse to wear them.
Land of 24-hour insomniacs, who
run their showers all night,
in hopes they might sleep to what sounds like rain.
Land where their idols don't care who they are,
where they're from, what they did,
as long as they love them.
Home of the high beams that blind from all directions,
but never pass or come any closer,
where you're family when you eat
at the restaurant chain, but anywhere
else you'll get whacked.
Where you lose things—wedding bands, celery sticks, sunglasses—
in the big box stores where you bought them,
where you hang your hat because they're furnished exactly
like your living room, stores
where more birds nest in the rafters than in trees.
The place where you live is "where you stay," and
where you say, when you visit your mom and dad,
"I'm going home,"
calling it still your mom and dad's,
even though your father's long gone.

Where there's a chicken in every pot
and a gun in every glove box,

nightstand, nursery, junk drawer, guest room, library, pool house,
greenhouse, conservatory…
Where everything, even butterflies,
like cats and cattle, is belled (freedom from fear),
and judges wield gavels like auctioneers,
and justice goes to the highest bidder.
Where no one knows after tears
how long eyes retain redness,
and no one's sure anymore if anyone's ever cried,
or whether they've never stopped.

AmeriKōans

The cut waters the glass.

The smoke boating the deck.

The stars driving the dark.

The wood backing the chop.

The abattoir fathering the snack.

The boat decking the smoke.

The laugh aspiring to listening.

Home limousines the wait.

The mortician founding the bargain.

The deck smoking the boat.

The drive darking the stars.

The chop wooding the back.

Waiting homes the limousine.

The magazine toileting time.

Water glassing the cut.

The bargain morticians the founding.

The Fathers, American and great-making.

The drowning practice Trumpeting,

Trumpeting the Donzerly light.

Vive les Vampires

About the vampires, this time,
I won't say a word. Same goes for
transience, same for loss.
So, weather: It wasn't, in fact, the humidity;
it was always about heat.
Only after Earth's cooling did fog rise,
Proterozoically, for the very first time.
Of the world's hard edges, a softening,
the likes of which we may not see in the future.
I imagine a pinewood box, red from rotting,
my father, his cufflinks, the tie clip ruined. Rot,
I can assure you, won't be mentioned again.
They say it's only homicide if you see it that way.
Vampires, they sure aren't biting each other.
At what point will the world run out of victims?
Multinational corporations, sending their condolences,
pretending to be my friends.
In the basement, somewhere, my mother is alive.
Dad, Dad, are you in there?
I forgive you for selective listening,
for your blind spots and prejudicial sight.
From the living room recliner, I release you.
Please, won't you come out?
O'Keeffe talked about the smallness of flowers—
how no one really sees them on account of their size.
To see, she said, takes time, and frankly, we're running out.

My father liked to tell me that his
was the most perfect bite the dentist had ever seen.
To prove it, I guess, he always brought home

the toughest cuts of meat.
Me: vegetarian at 16, braces at 45.
Cézanne said that the day would come
when a single carrot, freshly observed,
would set off a revolution.
Tenderness, I say, can be a revolution,
a distance from hoof and horn.
We live in a rainbow of chaos (Cézanne again),
but who says we couldn't use more Cézannes?
Along with skulls and flowers, O'Keeffe painted ladders,
floating, impossibly, between Earth and moon,
neither grounded nor a means of reaching the sublime.
Needing a ladder to reach a ladder, is that the human condition?
Who says the soul must leave the body?
It's not like checking for a heartbeat,
testing a door to see if it's hot.
If it's hot, by the way, don't open it.

The news reports that the zoo's giraffe
has fatally stepped on her newborn,
the calf unseen on account of its smallness.
Her neck, an impossible ladder,
a tenderness, between hoof and horn.
See that flower, smelling of rot? Who could miss it?
Same potential for ruin, recliner sized.
Critics always say art is about mortality,
a self-erected monument to the self,
a ladder to reach a ladder.
But critics have been known for their troubling
relationship with truth—and let's not even talk
about beauty.
For my preplanned, prepaid funeral,

I could not get a refund.
I showed them paintings, read them poems,
even told them I was planning to live forever.

Man vs. Himself

The story is being disassembled
for you and for me. Any flower
of at least three petals will be reverse engineered.
The tragedy still happens even if you tear out the last page.
Even if you step into the lobby, the violence still occurs,
            even if you look away.
Sometimes it happens offstage. Just ask Antigone, Agave, Iphigenia—
The plot has been drafted and erased so many times there's
a hole where words are supposed to be.
No one's surprised that it was all a dream (in fact, they're angry and tired).
The promise of an ending, an optimistic illusion:
cryptocurrency, non-fungible token,
a skin your digital self can wear.
Rain washes the wisteria.
Eurydice, don't even think about looking back.
The stone has already sealed the entrance.
The only way is forward.
The rain washing your car yesterday
is selling flood insurance today.
The best treatment for hubris
is to be looked at through the wrong end of binoculars.
There's a lesson here, a takeaway, if only the rain would stop,
if only we could find a story and a character foolish enough to deliver it.

Bildungsroman

I want to kiss your face
so I'm too close to see it.
Adult themes and situations,
beer cans and waterslides.
A nursery that's eerily quiet.
The anthropomorphic architecture of an orgy.
A job serving ice cream from an ice cream
shop in the shape of ice cream.
Skinny dipping in the tip jar.
Rapidly decreasing tolerance for cucumbers,
Lunchables, and hope.
Raccoons in the attic, possums
quite possibly in the walls.
Debriefings on the team-building trust exercises,
the requisite falling backward,
the requisite letting go.
Ask the moon about loss.
Illicit yawn in the calculus classroom,
being licked by a wave on Neptune.
Like Rembrandt rapping with Rubens.
Like too many cooks wrestling in the kitchen.
A duel is civilized if you're wearing a wig.
A preemptive, surgical brow lift.
Perpetually bewildered, perpetually surprised.
Beware of semelparous species,
that single reproductive episode before they die.
The comely bikinis of folk singers.
Lyrics like air conditioning, music like road noise.
The dune buggy idles, the bat rolls its eyes.
It's perpetually raining in your living room.
Sitting before the television,
your parents are always home.

Ars Poetica

Regrettably, the couple, comfortable with their growing
degree of satisfaction, came upon a large, seemingly friendly wolf
on their evening walk. The man thrust out a well-manicured hand
and grazed its mangy coat with his fingers, feeling something,
a boar bristle brush, maybe, or whiskered cheek, like my father's,
when nuzzled near mine. At the time the man and woman
were unspooled in a neoteric argument concerning their first
kiss, its cause and effect, who leaned in, how lust
did not necessarily end in love but sometimes marriage.
When the man called out to her, she turned
to see him touch the wolf. It was no tamer than a wasp,
but he coaxed it from the bush and touched its fur.
They watched to see if the wolf might follow
them up the road to the café or sink back toward
the boredom they had fled at home. Dust draped
the early evening light and swirled up around them.

"Regret" is a word that splits my heart.
The wolf must mean something,
just as the couple and my father must mean. Like the man,
I too want to reach down and stroke the animal,
wish to live allegorically, to play a part in this fable.
I want to run my fingers across its back,
brush the row of steel strings, until it howls at me.
I need to know how my father spent his last days
without eating my mother's meatloaf and mashed potatoes.
In which parts of your body did you feel pain,
I want to ask.

I was tasked with delivering mourners

from grief by speaking in sunflowers. But in truth,
words are not seeds or bullets. In the light one
sees that the dust is poisoned. Furrows of absolute silence,
couples sleeping in fields plowed with shame.
The heart makes a lousy instrument. That is to say,
it pumps no rage or fear until we hear our parents voice it.

They were never quite sure about the wolf afterward,
when they were home. What it was or whether
they saw it. Perhaps it wasn't a wolf at all
but a manifestation of mercy. Some creature
not worth their attention.

Morning-After Poem

It was lifeless. Last night, before the lights
were out, it failed to look under the bed.
It needed a chainsaw, a butcher knife, or
a baseball bat at least. So I stayed between
the sheets this morning, and after some surplus
sleep, I began to see it in a new light, as something
rising from freshly turned earth, a thing clawing
my imagination with the sight of pink flamingos
in a blizzard under a black light, a shotgun fired
in an empty train tunnel. I smelled it, as well,
along the nose of an Easter lily, a smoky liqueur
to my tongue. Scratching, rubbering, it had taken
hold of my pencil, and I surrendered.
It freed itself to the elbows and shoulders,
to the waist, then knees. I saw it thrash and shake
in the dirt like a dancer performing a heart attack
for the stage, convincing at least one of us to call 9-1-1.

Glissando (the Descending Kind)

...out of the easily infinite,
mortality:
slide whistle (& bells)
   February,
flameless votives
mortalenemiesrivalsfollowersfriends
(batteries NOT incl)

you surrender unwinking
to hairpin turns
thigh-thick shades of blue
   twilight, breath baited
for the rodent-hued dawn

unwincingly you
stumble   you
out of the tinysmall
chartreuse arrival
crawl, prayingly

Why am I?
the because life
   most likely unmade of
praise & daffodils

of howdy-do's & sunrise

Ctrl+Alt+Del

You quit the cursor, the drive to town, the rain
at noon, the glue and gasoline that *got your nose.*

And the ritual of late, of pothole and pitch—
torn, mangled, stitched out of rage or envy.

Almost, give up the *almost,* the *nearly,* and *not quite.*
Retire, undistinguished members of the *just shy.*
Quit your elephantine *about,*
and whatever filled your tank but left it empty.

Surrender the pistol that triggers the rifle
that fires the cannon that launches grenades.
Ignite the fuse of memory. Memory
is no act of terror. It can't win wars,
is not a weapon. Forgetting isn't a crime.

At dusk, the rain is without enemies, the roads
you drive or not. The throbbing cursor feels no love
for the letter, word, or sentence. Punctuation
can't comprehend its own sentence.
You can't comprehend your sentence either.

Evenings are hands still, closed eyes,
are the fan's noise, hushed
by the *can'ts, won'ts,* and *nevers.*

You watch for clouds when it's clear,
seek a clearing when it's clouds,
each road, a composition played by car tires.
The replica you who does your bidding.

Humane//Society: Vegan Fail III

The refrigerator in the breakroom grew
disillusioned and bored with the mind-
numbing work of chilling my lunches—
it grumbled and sighed, groaned and cried
before it quit altogether without tendering notice.

I told myself the milk was still fresh,
raised a glass of it in a show of solidarity:

To the mayonnaise that spoiled
the planet, the yogurt that poisoned
the world, to the eggs that fouled the earth,
making omnivores and vegetarians feel ashamed.

And now I've spoiled my appetite;
there's none but the one for destruction:
for the shelling of the chicken coop,
the air strike on the pasture,
for the hand-to-hand combat and
friendly fire in the trophic war
I wage against myself.

En Masse: Provincetown

I. *Private Property*

The couple sits on the beach—
the woman faces the bay, the man, the sun, setting on the town.
Like police cruisers they are parked
in identical lawn chairs—
the kind that last for just one season.

II. *Hostel: No Outlet*

Decide between the nightlight or the window unit,
the sound of crickets, bladed in the fan, or the smell of electrified dust.
Give me back my eyelids, or at least my privacy—
or be warned: I can take it,
I can take them back myself.

III. *Low Tide*

The beach is a sand orphan, many men, none smiling,
biceps bulging from shirtsleeves. One weeds a wife
from the wine-red zinnias. The Sunday school
is held at the end of the dock at a bar. Here women sing, their voices
rising like a toast to God. The bay is a rubber tire,
its tread worn off, and we all become nails, square heads,
always certain of the claw-ended hammer.

IV. *To Be Shouted Into a Megaphone*

Please pet the German shepherds!
Anyone found without a manicure will be waltzed off to the salon!

Those without cupcakes will be given electric blankets!
If you don't have a ticket, you may fly in the easy chair!
No one has to choose between sprinkles and glitter!
Any cars parked on the moon will be towed at the expense of God!

V. *New Arrival*

One long, followed by three short blasts from the ferry—no S.O.S., no stress,
    just So.

VI. *Please Recycle*

Two trash cans, evergreen, empty, have been wheeled side by side.
They're keeping each other company.
A lone recycling bin. Its arrows, white. They point at each other,
bent in an endless triangle of recrimination.

VII. *Exhaust*

Two men, red cups thrust before them:
happy hour high beams cut through rush hour traffic.

VIII. *Empathy*

Both eyes will tear, even when only one is injured,
the molars will ache for the rotten incisor.
Two poodles barking, one favoring its back leg,
while the other sniffs its ass.

Harp

Under a lean-to in the desert, a man plays the harp.
The harp would prefer not to be played like basketball.
It doesn't want him to snatch at its strings
like a power forward until the sound is fouled.
But the man swarms the harp, enters it
like waxwings flying in fruit trees.
They crash into windows, drunk on wine, stunning
themselves against memory and birdsong.
The harp would rather play disposal choked with beer caps
or teacher holding the world record for loudest
with her shout of the word *quiet.*
The harp wants to play lizard lifting one foot, then another
from scorching rocks. It wants to roll over and sleep.
Wants to drink vodka and lime with a splash of tonic.
The harp would like to see the man with his lover, and
what he does with his hands. It would like to bat its eyes
at the bats flying from caves at twilight.
The harp wants to be an accountant. It wants to play economically.
At 35 after, it wants to bill for the entire hour.
It wants to wear wingtips in bed.
It would like to play every note at the same time,
steel cable of sound spiraling through its blood.
The harp asks the man to remember the first time he heard harp
and the first sound he played, envy, as he sat at the teacher's elbow.
The man claims not to remember the tune, considers instead
the cactus blooming pinkly at his feet.
The harp wants to blow the blue sky clear of its only cloud.
It would love to roll in the dust,
shake itself off and laugh with madness.
The harp would like to erase forgiveness from the man's future—

and the potential to be forgiven.

It wants to hiccup in time with the music, to play sunbursts
and solar flares and the stalactites dripping, growing inch by inch
in caverns underground. It wants to play the man's three gray hairs,
and the age spots developing on the backs of his hands.

The harp wants the man to curtsy in his caftan.

It wants him to hear Coltrane and (for once) think *Alice* not *John*.

It wants him to wander the desert, hunting rabbits
until he reaches a burrow and babies.

It wants him to pull a top hat from inside.

Yes, it wants that kind of magic.

The harp is frightened of the man's hands, riot of anxiety.

Sandstorm, curse of the wind. The harp worries about the man,
inflation, and genocide. It wants to hold up a sign and march
into the village shouting its demands.

It would rather the man be played, to make noise of his body.

Sneeze. Slapped thigh: something percussive, something wind.

He may not recognize this music if he stops playing the harp.

He may think the audience is weeping, not dabbing sand from their eyes.

The Governor Asks Us to Pray for Rain

The wind borrows its walk from a drunk.
It is "very warm."
A car sets sail on a retention pond
and actually goes pretty far.
Stupid sunset. Stupid, spectacular sunrise.
Succulents clinging to baked dirt,
tumbleweeds letting go.
It's no wonder I can't think clearly:
chlorophyll clogging the synapses—greener days behind.
Who looks at a thumbprint and can recognize themselves?
The supernova aspires to be a soul,
not the same old stardust.
The coyote wants to be a cathedral,
the lizard wants wings.
Subatomic particles only act benign
in bodies of benign people.
Iffy, like hydrating, water-enhancing electrolytes,
iffy, like overeating at a wake.
Who's pulling the feeding tube from the clouds?
When you look through the eyes of a crocodile,
you develop a reptilian point of view.
I get it, squinting out into desert,
my mouth is small and singular
and speaks with a foreign tongue.
I know now that God can't hear me, know
that God's not listening.

Rave On

All hip, all thigh, entirely darker now than dirt.

We could pin you to earth   our dance

      could bury you. Arabesque, plié,

tremble before us,   whimper   while we still have
ears.

A storm thunders in,   chills our breath to cloud,

      disappears our faces,   our heads.

We the wine,   our bodies

giving it shape, our dance. A river,

      upstream, the origin of poison,   source of decay.

For you, fists   sleep in our fingers, kicks

      lie dormant in our legs. Sad,

sorry plié   we danced your bones until the hammer fell

      then kept dancing. We the tongueless,   the merci-
less we.

A dog snarls with all three heads,

a god hammering earth, endlessly   splitting it open.

      Do you see us oozing from fissures

      and faults? Blood bright, molten,

our hips   comprise their own nation, thighs

a country unto themselves: republic of *you're-not-welcome*,

dominion of un-belong.

No Context

At 5:00 a.m., under the red line platform in Ambler Heights,
you can't see the river, sunrise breaking across the water, sunshine
warming the sandstone of the Hope Memorial Bridge.
Unseen from here are its sandstone carvings, those
Art Deco guardians of promise, progress, and industry.
There is a man on the street who looks
as if his will has been ransomed.
A deposed king in demolition boots,
his coat resembling a mastodon hide.
Ice age, king dethroned, yet another mammal
on the verge of extinction.

Here, at 5:00 a.m., under the platform of the red line,
it feels as though nothing is possible.
Here, no one ever called brushing your teeth, flopping
on a mattress post–third shift, a prelude to a beautiful dream.
I'm so goddamned god-damned and defeated
I can't believe no one has asked me to marry them.
In Ambler nobody is made in the image of god.

Good morning, people of the platform, lost
on your way to—or from—work in clouds
of your own making, pot smoke, frozen breath,
your own private microclimate.
Good morning beatboxers, and to everyone:
sellers of loose cigarettes, of aluminum and copper
wire, and to those leaning on windows, still asleep,
and those propped up in the bus stop shelter.

"False friends," my high school teacher called them:
vague and *wave*, *gift* and *poison*, *pain* and *pain*,
two words, imposters, one posing as another.

False friends, true enemies, all the same.
Close and *close*, *tear* and *tear*, *wound* and *wound*,
these they call heteronyms. Impossible
to say without context, like how it's
cold and dark at 5:00 a.m., and hard to say
why I'm standing here in the absence of context,
living my life without reference.

I recently learned about contranyms, words like *dust, fix, apology*.
Dust can mean to both add and remove particles:
> *Clouds dust the street with snow;*
> *wind dusts the snow away.*

Murder in the first degree is the worst
but is the mildest when used to describe a burn.
The Hope Memorial Bridge does not, as the name implies,
memorialize the loss of hope, that naïve and childish longing,
nor was it named to instill it.
Hope refers to the father of the famous entertainer,
a man lesser known for his stonemasonry.
When I say, "I'm finished," how I wish I meant
that I've completed or accomplished something.
But when I say it now, "I'm finished,"
it means I'm completely done for.

ACKNOWLEDGMENTS

Grateful acknowledgment to the following publications in which poems from this collection first appeared or are forthcoming:

Antioch Review
Baltimore Review
Bayou Magazine
Cincinnati Review
Cola Literary Review
Copper Nickel
Denver Quarterly
descant
The Fiddlehead
Frontier Poetry
Gettysburg Review
Grist: A Journal of the Literary Arts
International Poetry Review
The MacGuffin
The McNeese Review
The Midwest Quarterly
The Minnesota Review
The Missouri Review
New American Writing
New England Review
North American Review
Plume
Poet Lore
Redivider
So to Speak
The South Carolina Review
Sou'wester
Spillway
Spoon River Poetry Review
The Threepenny Review
TriQuarterly
Verse Daily
Western Humanities Review
WomenArts Quarterly Journal

ABOUT THE AUTHOR

Cindy King is the author of a book-length poetry collection, *Zoonotic* (2022), and two poetry chapbooks, *Easy Street* (2021) and *Lesser Birds of Paradise* (2022). Her poems have appeared or are forthcoming in *The Sun, Prairie Schooner, Gettysburg Review, The Threepenny Review, North American Review, Denver Quarterly, Cincinnati Review*, and elsewhere. She has received fellowships and scholarships from Tin House, Sewannee, and the Fine Arts Work Center. Cindy was born in Cleveland, Ohio, and grew up swimming in the shadows of the hyperboloid cooling towers on the shores of Lake Erie. She is a professor of creative writing at Utah Tech University and faculty editor of *The Southern Quill* and *Route 7 Review*. She is an editorial assistant for *TriQuarterly* and *Seneca Review*.